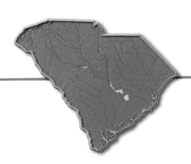

THE PALMETTO STATE

by Ann Volkwein

Curriculum Consultant: Jean Craven,
Director of Instructional Support,
Albuquerque, NM, Public Schools

WORLD ALMANAC® LIBRARY

Please visit our web site at: **www.worldalmanaclibrary.com**
For a free color catalog describing World Almanac® Library's
list of high-quality books and multimedia programs, call
1-800-848-2928 (USA) or 1-800-387-3178 (Canada).
World Almanac® Library's fax: (414) 332-3567.

Library of Congress Cataloging-in-Publication Data

Volkwein, Ann.
    South Carolina, the Palmetto State / by Ann Volkwein.
        p. cm. — (World Almanac Library of the states)
    Includes bibliographical references and index.
    Summary: Examines the history, people, land, economy and commerce,
politics and government, culture, notable people, and state events and attractions
of South Carolina.
    ISBN 0-8368-5144-7 (lib. bdg.)
    ISBN 0-8368-5314-8 (softcover)
    1. South Carolina—Juvenile literature. [1. South Carolina.] I. Title. II. Series.
F269.3.V65   2002
975.7—dc21   2002071502

This edition first published in 2002 by
World Almanac® Library
330 West Olive Street, Suite 100
Milwaukee, WI 53212 USA

This edition © 2002 by World Almanac® Library.

Design and Editorial: Bill SMITH STUDIO Inc.
Editor: Timothy Paulson
Assistant Editor: Megan Elias
Art Director: Olga Lamm
Photo Research: Sean Livingstone
World Almanac® Library Project Editor: Patricia Lantier
World Almanac® Library Editors: Monica Rausch, Mary Dykstra, Lyman Lyons
World Almanac® Library Production: Tammy Gruenewald, Katherine A. Goedheer

Photo credits: pp. 4-5 © PhotoDisc; p. 6 (bottom) © CORBIS, (top) © PhotoSpin; p. 7 (top)
© ArtToday, (bottom) © Library of Congress; p. 9 © Library of Congress; p. 10 South Carolina
Dept. of Parks, Recreation and Tourism; p. 11 © Dover; p. 12 © Library of Congress; p. 13
© Dover; p. 15 © CORBIS; p. 17 © Library of Congress; p. 18 South Carolina Dept. of Parks,
Recreation and Tourism; p. 20 (all) South Carolina Dept. of Parks, Recreation and Tourism; p. 21
(left to right) © Corel, South Carolina Dept. of Parks, Recreation and Tourism, © CORBIS; p. 23
© Corel; p. 26 © PhotoDisc; p. 27 South Carolina Dept. of Parks, Recreation and Tourism; p. 29
© Library of Congress; p. 31 (all) © Library of Congress; p. 32 South Carolina Dept. of Parks,
Recreation and Tourism; p. 33 South Carolina Dept. of Parks, Recreation and Tourism; p. 34
South Carolina Dept. of Parks, Recreation and Tourism; p. 35 © Dover; p. 36 South Carolina Dept.
of Parks, Recreation and Tourism; p. 37 © Tami Chappel/Reuters/TimePix; p. 38 © PhotoDisc;
p. 39 © Allan Grant/TimePix; p. 40 © PhotoDisc; p. 41 © Greg Mathieson/MAI/TimePix; pp. 42-43
© Library of Congress; p. 44 (top) South Carolina Dept. of Parks, Recreation and Tourism,
(bottom) © PhotoDisc; p. 45 South Carolina Dept. of Parks, Recreation and Tourism

Printed in the United States of America

1 2 3 4 5 6 7 8 9 06 05 04 03 02

South Carolina

Carolina on Our Minds

For many, the mention of South Carolina conjures romantic images of vast plantations, hoopskirts, and Spanish moss hanging lazily from the branches of giant live oaks. Others see pristine beaches and manicured golf courses, all with the flavor of a bygone era. Indeed, the past hangs near and heavy in this small southern state; the very shape of the land created a tug-of-war that lasted for centuries and eventually helped spark this nation's Civil War.

The long-running dispute among settlers had its roots in the physical division of South Carolina's countryside. The vast differences between the rugged mountains of the Up Country and the fertile coastal plains of the Low Country encouraged the political division between the subsistence farmers in the hills and the powerful, wealthy plantation owners below.

The plantation owners, called planters, favored slavery and created a furor as the national government appeared to be moving against this institution. The planters' anger escalated, and South Carolina became the first state to secede from the Union, firing the first shots of the Civil War at Fort Sumter.

Only in recent decades has South Carolina begun to reclaim the prosperity it had prior to Reconstruction. The battle for civil rights was a long one here, fought over such issues as voting rights and school desegregation. But despite the trials of the twentieth century, South Carolinians remain close to the past and close to their state; 75 percent are born, live, and die here.

Today, residents are mainly employed by the manufacturing and tourism industries. Visitors are drawn to the grandeur of the plantation museums and gardens, the richness of the Gullah culture of the Sea Islands, the broad sand beaches and golf courses of the Grand Strand, and Revolutionary and Civil War monuments. Crisscrossed by history, South Carolina is wealthy in both tradition and pride.

▶ Map of South Carolina showing the interstate highway system, as well as major cities and waterways.

▼ The tree-lined approach to Boone Hall Plantation in Mount Pleasant.

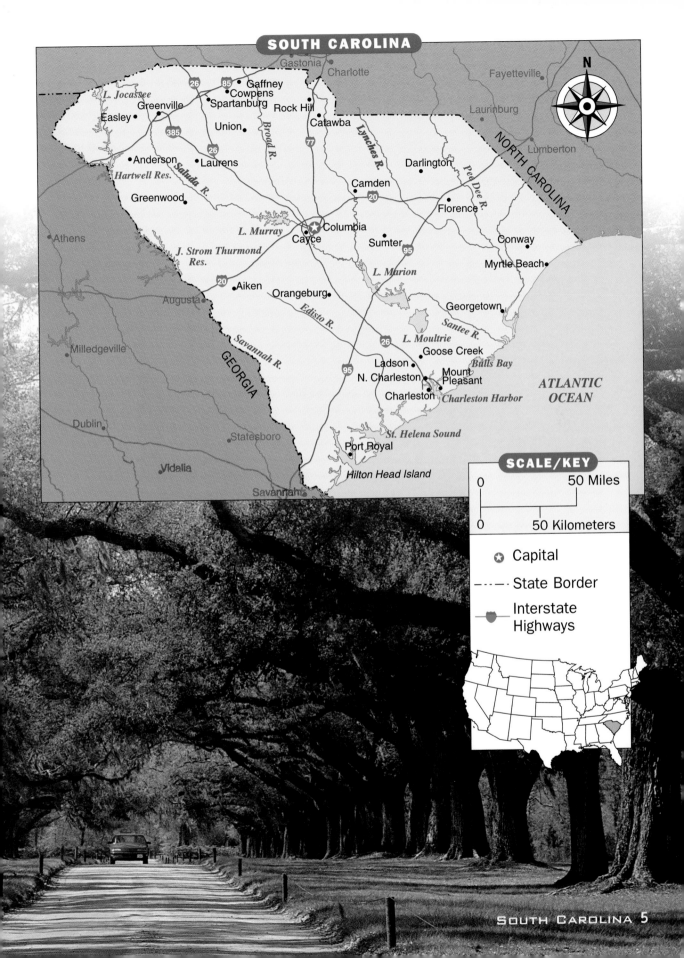

Gastonia

Fayetteville

Charlotte

L. Jocassee

26

85

Gaffney

Cowpens

Spartanburg

Rock Hill

Laurinburg

Greenville

Easley

Union

Catawba

385

Lynches R.

NORTH CAROLINA

Lumberton

Darlington

Anderson

26

Laurens

Brood R.

77

Hartwell Res.

Saluda R.

Camden

Pee Dee R.

Greenwood

20

Florence

Conway

L. Murray

Columbia

J. Strom Thurmond Res.

Cayce

Sumter

95

Myrtle Beach

L. Marion

Athens

20

Aiken

Orangeburg

Savannah R.

Edisto R.

Santee R.

Georgetown

GEORGIA

26

L. Moultrie

Goose Creek

Bulls Bay

Milledgeville

95

Ladson

N. Charleston

Mount Pleasant

ATLANTIC OCEAN

Charleston

Charleston Harbor

Dublin

St. Helena Sound

Statesboro

Port Royal

Vidalia

Hilton Head Island

Savannah

N

SCALE/KEY

0 ——————— 50 Miles

0 ——————— 50 Kilometers

★ Capital

– · – · – State Border

Interstate Highways

Fast Facts

South Carolina (SC), The Palmetto State

Entered Union

May 23, 1788 (8th state)

Capital   **Population**

Columbia 116,278

Total Population (2000)

4,012,012 (26th most populous state)
— *Between 1990 and 2000, population
increased by 15.1 percent.*

Largest Cities   **Population**

Columbia 116,278
Charleston 96,650
North Charleston 79,641
Greenville 56,002

Land Area

30,109 square miles (77,982 square
kilometers) (40th largest state)

State Motto

"Dum Spiro Spero" *and* "Animis
Opibusque Parati" — *Both are in
Latin. The first means* "While I
Breathe I Hope" *and the second*
"Ready in Soul and Resource."

State Song

"Carolina," *words by Henry Timrod,
music by Anne Custis Burgess,
adopted in 1911, and* "South
Carolina on My Mind," *by
Hank Martin and Buzz
Arledge, adopted in 1984.*

State Animal

White-tailed deer

State Bird

Carolina wren

State Fish

Striped bass

State Insect

Carolina mantid (praying mantis) —
*Mantids eat other
insects that are
harmful to crops.*

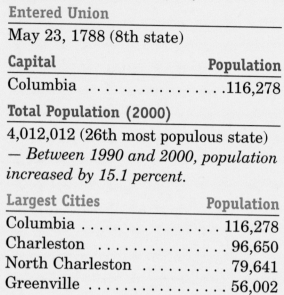

State Tree

Palmetto — *During the
Revolutionary War, South Carolina
defeated the British from a fort built
of palmetto logs on Sullivans Island.*

State Flower

Yellow jessamine

State Shell

Lettered olive

State Gem

Amethyst — *Some of the finest
amethysts in the United States
are mined in South Carolina.*

State Fruit

Peach

State Dance

Shag — *Rhythm and blues gave birth
to this regional dance, which can be
performed to virtually any tempo.*

State Beverage

Milk

State Reptile

Loggerhead sea turtle

State Wild Game Bird

Wild turkey

Myrtle Beach, *The Grand Strand*

Broad white-sand beaches, golf, tennis, and a lively music scene attract visitors to this coastal city. It's a short drive to quainter coastal areas, parks, and gardens.

Magnolia Plantation, *Charleston*

Magnificent gardens surround this plantation house, including the Audubon Swamp Garden. Although the original house was "Shermanized," or burned to the ground, the existing mansion was brought downriver by the family and placed on the original foundation.

Darlington Raceway, *Darlington*

Home to the National Association of Stock Car Auto Racing (NASCAR) TranSouth Financial 400 as well as the Mountain Dew Southern 500, the Darlington Raceway is hallowed ground for auto-racing fans. The Stock Car Hall of Fame is located next door.

For other places and events, see p. 44.

BIGGEST, BEST, AND MOST

- The town of Sumter is the home of the largest ginkgo farm in the world.

- In 1996, Senator Strom Thurmond became the oldest person ever to hold a U.S. Senate seat and the longest-serving senator in U.S. history.

- Totaling more than 700 feet (213 meters), the highest series of cascades in eastern America are the Whitewater Falls on the South Carolina/North Carolina border.

STATE FIRSTS

- **1786** A group of Scottish merchants founded the first golf club in the nation, the South Carolina Golf Club, in Charleston.

- **1860** South Carolina was the first state to secede from the Union.

- **1861** The first shot of the Civil War was fired at Fort Sumter in Charleston on April 12.

Dueling President

South Carolina native President Andrew Jackson was involved in many duels in his time. During a duel with Charles Dickinson in 1806 over an insult to Jackson's wife, Dickinson fired first and wounded Jackson in the chest. As rules dictated, Dickinson was forced to stand his ground as the wounded Jackson aimed again, killing his opponent. The bullet that wounded Jackson was never removed.

Endless Rice Paddies

In the 1840s, slave labor in Georgetown produced almost half the rice grown in the United States. In the 1840 census, 88 percent of the population of Georgetown County were slaves, most of them engaged in growing rice. The work of clearing out cypress swamps using hand tools was brutal, and the life expectancy of a slave was just nineteen years. Planters preferred to use women slaves, who endured the swamp conditions better than the men. The monumental task of building hundreds of square miles of rice paddies, which was done by digging ditches and drainage systems, has been compared to the work of building the Great Pyramids of Egypt.

▲ A pre-Civil War rice mill.

The Heart of Dixie

> Let the South Carolinians of another generation remember that the state taught them how to live and how to die.
>
> — *excerpt from the Monument to the Confederate Dead in Columbia*

The rolling hills, coastal plains, and river deltas of South Carolina have been inhabited for eleven to twelve thousand years. The earliest groups were hunters and gatherers. Peoples of the Mississippian culture, known for their temple mounds and complex social structure, arrived in approximately A.D. 1100. The earthen mounds they left behind can still be seen today in the South Carolina countryside.

By the time Europeans arrived in North America, the Cherokee, Catawba, and Yamasee Native American nations, among many others, were thriving in the region that would become South Carolina. Contact with Europeans, beginning with a series of failed Spanish and French Protestant settlements in the sixteenth century, brought death to substantial numbers of Native Americans through armed conflict and infectious diseases. Many Yamasee and Cherokee had been driven out or had left by the end of the Revolutionary War. In 1838, the U.S. government forced all members of the Cherokee nation to leave their homeland and walk the infamous Trail of Tears to territory in Oklahoma. Today, the Catawba have a small reservation within the state. They were awarded $50 million by the government in 1993 as a settlement for legal claims.

Native Americans of South Carolina

- Catawba
- Cherokee
- Chicora
- Combahee
- Cusabo
- Edisto
- Etiwan
- Kiawah
- Pee Dee
- Waccamaw
- Yamasee

Colonization

The first Europeans to sight South Carolina's shores were the Spanish, in the early sixteenth century. The earliest settlement, led by Lucas Vasquez de Ayllon in 1526, survived only a few months, only to be followed by another failed settlement attempt by French Protestants. Finally, in 1566, a group of Spanish settlers managed to set up a lasting community on Parris Island, which remained until 1587,

DID YOU KNOW?

South Carolina was named for Charles I, the first English king to charter the land.

when they abandoned it for St. Augustine, Florida. Control of the land between present-day Virginia and Florida then fell to England, whose king, Charles II, granted it to eight noblemen in 1663. These Lords Proprietors, as they were called, controlled the area that would one day be North Carolina and South Carolina, as well as part of northern Georgia.

In 1670, Lord Anthony Ashley Cooper, one of the eight noblemen, led a group of English settlers to Albemarle Point. The settlers eventually chose Oyster Point — later Charles Town and today Charleston — as their home. The Lords Proprietors appointed by Charles II had full control over the structure of the lives of the colonists, as well as financial interests in the venture.

By the late 1600s, the colonists had begun to trade with Native Americans for furs, which they exported to pay for their colony's expansion. Meanwhile, Barbadian planters settled in the colony in large numbers, bringing slave labor — mostly from West Africa — and the knowledge of rice cultivation.

The rice crop and fur trade together made the Carolina colony very profitable. Nevertheless, the colonists were not satisfied with the policies of the proprietary rulers. They felt open to attack from all quarters — Native Americans, French, Spanish, and pirates alike. In 1715, the colonists went to war with the Yamasee. Then, in 1718, the pirate Blackbeard threatened to attack Charles Town. Although all he wanted was medicine, rather than the usual gold, it was still unsettling. The colonists rebelled against the proprietors in 1719 by buying the colony from them and giving control of it to the British king. The colony of North Carolina was already being ruled separately by this time. South Carolina officially became a royal province, governed and protected by the British crown, in 1729.

In 1732, the king founded the colony of Georgia to the southwest of South Carolina. Georgia served as a buffer between South Carolina and Spanish-controlled Florida.

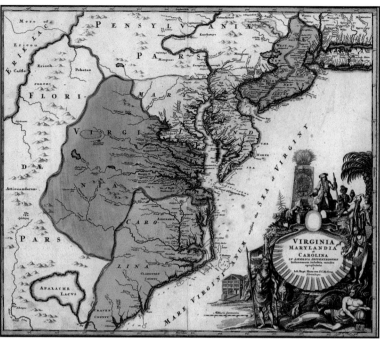

▲ This map of Virginia, Maryland, and the Carolinas was created by a European mapmaker around 1759.

Slave Revolt

On September 9, 1739, the first major slave insurrection in North America occurred at the Stono River plantations in South Carolina. The slaves were inspired by a rumor that the Spanish were granting freedom to slaves in St. Augustine. Twenty whites and forty African Americans died in the revolt.

During the 1750s, the Piedmont region, or Up Country, was settled, and by the late eighteenth century, Charles Town was thriving. As settlers established farms, rice and indigo became major sources of wealth. Both crops were grown on large plantations, and their profitability was ensured by slave labor.

Revolution and Statehood

Despite the prosperity found under British rule, South Carolina ultimately joined the twelve other rebellious colonies in the Revolutionary War. Planters' sons, educated in England, felt prepared to govern themselves, and the taxes imposed by the British inspired Charles Town's very own version of the famous Boston Tea Party. In March 1776, an independent South Carolina government was set up, with John Rutledge as governor. That same year, South Carolina sent four delegates to the Continental Congress in Philadelphia. Edward Rutledge, Thomas Hayward, Jr., Thomas Lynch, Jr., and Arthur Middleton signed the Declaration of Independence for South Carolina.

There were many Revolutionary War battles within the state, with major ones taking place at Kings Mountain and Cowpens. During the war, the British occupied Charles Town from 1780 to 1782. When the colonists gained control in 1783, the town was renamed Charleston.

DID YOU KNOW?

The U.S. Census of 1790 counted 249,073 people in South Carolina, of whom 107,094 were slaves.

DID YOU KNOW?

During the Revolutionary War, more battles were fought in South Carolina than in any other state.

▼ At the Battle of Kings Mountain in 1780 (reenacted here), patriots routed colonists who were loyal to the British Crown.

Although Charleston had served as the colony's capital and major port, the South Carolina government decided to choose a new site for a capital in 1786. The city of Columbia was founded in the center of the state in an attempt to balance competing economic interests, including the small farms of the rugged Up Country and the expansive plantations of the flatter Low Country.

On May 23, 1788, South Carolina became the eighth state to ratify the Constitution of the United States. In 1790, the state adopted a charter that provided residents with religious freedom. Only men who owned property were eligible to vote or hold elected office, however. Furthermore, a voter had an additional three-fifths vote for each slave he owned. These laws ensured that the planters were in control of the sate legislature.

In 1793, the cotton gin was invented, making the cultivation of cotton extremely profitable. The cotton "gin" — short for "engine" — quickly removed seeds from cotton bolls. Formerly, this had been a very labor-intensive, and therefore expensive, task. Cotton quickly became one of South Carolina's major cash crops.

By 1800, cotton plantations had begun to appear in the Piedmont region, creating more of a balance between Up Country interests and those of the Low Country. The hilly Piedmont region had not allowed rice growing, and the better-suited cotton crop allowed Up Country farmers to operate on a plantation scale for the first time. As a result, slave ownership rose in the Up Country, giving these farmers a stronger voice in the governing of the state.

Railroads, canals, and roads linked parts of the state, funneling Up Country crops to Charleston where they were exported. The first commercial railroad in the nation debuted in Charleston on December 25, 1830. The line would eventually extend from Charleston to Hamburg.

John Caldwell Calhoun

Raised in Abbeville, John Caldwell Calhoun (1782–1850) was from a moderately successful Up Country family. Educated at Yale and Litchfield Law School, he entered Congress before he was thirty years old. Calhoun was secretary of war from 1817 to 1825, serving under President James Monroe. He was elected vice president under John Quincy Adams in 1824, and again in 1828 under Andrew Jackson. In 1828, when several Southern states objected to a high tariff designed to help Northern states, Calhoun argued that they should be allowed to ignore it. This was known as the Nullification Crisis. Calhoun believed that when the interests of a state conflicted with the interests of the nation, the state's interests should come first. In 1832, Calhoun was elected to the U.S. Senate, and he quit the vice presidency to serve as South Carolina's senator.

Seeds of War

The cotton gin made it possible for Southern farmers to plant more cotton than they ever had before. This machine took time and cost out of processing the crop, and it suddenly made sense to grow as much as possible. Soon, so much cotton was being produced that the price went down. The farmers' solution was to produce still more cotton to make up for the low price. This increased production required more slaves, which increased costs and cut into profits. This cycle would continue for years, undermining the South's economy.

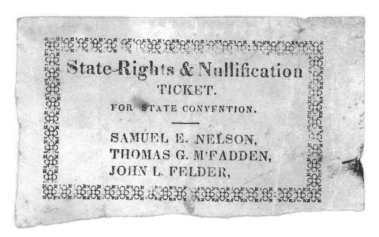

During the War of 1812, the U.S. government placed higher taxes on exported goods to raise money for the war. The Northern lawmakers continued this trend after the war, placing tariffs on the South's main crop, cotton, as well as on all other exports and imports. This action forced the South to buy its manufactured goods from the North and essentially punished the South for selling its goods in Europe. Dissension grew, prompting many South Carolinian planters to talk of breaking off, or seceding, from the Union.

In 1828, an even higher tariff was put in place. In response, South Carolina passed the 1832 Ordinance of Nullification, which said that South Carolina refused to obey the tariff laws. Vice President John C. Calhoun, a South Carolinian, led the argument that no state was bound by a law the state regarded as unconstitutional. At the time, no other Southern states followed South Carolina's lead. Meanwhile, South Carolina native President Andrew Jackson condemned this practice, called nullification. The state ordinance was repealed in 1833 and a compromise was reached, but the battle made certain divisions clear. On one side were those who believed that the Union — the United States of America — had to be preserved, with the federal government having the final say. On the other side were supporters of states' rights, those who believed that the power of the federal government should not be greater than that of each individual state. Calhoun was a strong proponent of states' rights, and he also became a spokesman for the South.

▲ The issue of nullification — states ignoring federal law and going their own way — would become a critical step on the road to civil war.

Multi-purpose

The Charleston structure that is now known as the Old Exchange and Provost Dungeon has played a variety of important roles in South Carolina's history. It was an indoor market, a customs warehouse, a meeting place for American revolutionaries, a British prison, and a post office. In 1825, an almanac declared it the best and most convenient post office in America.

The nullification battle brought another division to light — the nation's attitude toward slavery. The rise of Northern abolitionist (or anti-slavery) sentiments and the debate in Congress over whether new U.S. territories should allow slavery struck fear in the hearts of plantation owners throughout the state.

Civil War

On December 20, 1860, South Carolina became the first state to secede from the Union. Abraham Lincoln had just been elected president, and his Republican party strongly opposed the spread of slavery. Lincoln had won the election without a single electoral vote from a Southern state. Most Southerners believed that Lincoln's election meant the end of any national political influence for Southern states and the end of the Southern way of life. An anti-abolitionist radical from South Carolina named Robert Barnwell Rhett led the Southern resistance. The views Rhett represented would ultimately solidify Southern states into a unified Confederate front.

On April 12, 1861, Confederate troops fired upon Union-held Fort Sumter in Charleston Harbor. This event marked the beginning of the Civil War. More than sixty thousand South Carolinians joined the Confederate Army, and nearly one-fourth would lose their lives by the war's end. The worst destruction within the state came in 1865 when,

▼ Throughout the Civil War, Union army forces bombarded Charleston. By 1865, when this picture was taken, much of the city was in ruins. The steeple in the background belongs to St. Philips Church, home to the oldest congregation in Charleston.

after marching through Georgia, General William T. Sherman led his troops on a swath of destruction through South Carolina. He ended his march by burning the city of Columbia.

Reconstruction

After the Civil War, South Carolina grew to resent federal interference, as the U.S. government began what was called Reconstruction, or the rebuilding of the South. This bitterness lasted for decades, as federal forces imposed governmental changes on the South. Many of those who had power in Confederate South Carolina held onto power after the war was over. They refused to let African Americans vote. The U.S. government responded by sending in federal troops and requiring that South Carolina grant voting rights to all men regardless of race before the state could rejoin the Union. South Carolina was readmitted to the Union in 1868.

After federal troops left the state in 1877, a group of planters, lawyers, and merchants known as the Bourbon Democrats took control of the government. They got their nickname because they were as conservative and autocratic as the Bourbon dynasty that had ruled France before its revolution in 1789. The Bourbon Democrats were against granting civil rights to African Americans. By the mid-1890s, South Carolina had passed the so-called "Jim Crow" laws, which segregated schools and other facilities and made it hard for African Americans to vote.

The Twentieth and Twenty-First Centuries

In the early part of the twentieth century, South Carolina's economy was hard hit. First, a hurricane destroyed the state's rice plantations, which never recovered. Then, in the early 1920s, the boll weevil, an insect pest, devastated the cotton crop. Meanwhile, soil erosion caused farms to fail, so many farmers and low-wage agricultural workers left the state for northern cities. The textile industry, having blossomed in the 1890s, became the state's primary industry. New England companies, attracted by South Carolina's rushing rivers and cheap labor, opened water-powered mills.

During American involvement in World War I, from 1917 to 1918, the status of African Americans in South Carolina improved somewhat as they served in the armed forces and

South for Sale

A 1911 hurricane permanently devastated the South Carolina rice plantations, and the boll weevil ruined the Sea Island cotton plantations in 1922. As a result, nearly 1 million acres (404,678 hectares) of Low Country plantation land changed hands in a three-week period in 1925. By 1940, wealthy northerners owned 159 of the region's original plantations, using them as retreats and hunting lodges.

worked in war-related industries. After the war ended, however, a wave of violence against African Americans, mostly caused by racist groups, swept through the South, driving many African Americans to leave the state. By 1930, the majority of South Carolina's population was white.

FOR THE SUNNY SOUTH

▲ This cartoon from 1913 parodies the South's Jim Crow laws, under which African Americans were forced to use separate facilities and modes of transportation.

In 1929, the stock market crashed and the Great Depression began. The textile industry in South Carolina suffered, as did the state's farmers. The state had so little income that it had to pay teachers' salaries in promissory notes.

World War II revived the state's economy, particularly giving a boost to manufacturing. Soybean, tobacco, and peach crops increased as well, and employment picked up in the 1950s. Southern culture, however, remained resistant to change. It wasn't until 1947 that African Americans were allowed to vote in the Democratic primaries, and laws requiring them to pay a tax in order to vote weren't lifted until the mid-1950s.

In 1954, the U.S. Supreme Court declared school segregation illegal in *Brown v. Board of Education of Topeka, Kansas*. Segregation was a social system in which African Americans and whites supposedly had "separate but equal" access to public places and schools. It wasn't until 1963 that schools in South Carolina began to be integrated.

Racial integration was pushed to the forefront by federal legislation, as well as by protests. One of the most famous of these demonstrations was the 1968 Orangeburg Massacre, in which three African Americans were killed and twenty-seven others were injured by state police officers. In 1969, a legislative committee recommended changes to the 1895 state constitution, and in the early 1970s, new articles were adopted, conforming to federal laws.

Today, as the twenty-first century opens, the tourist industry and investors, attracted by low taxes, help brighten the financial future for the once-troubled state.

Born and Bred in South Carolina

> We, like the Chinese, eat rice and worship
> our ancestors.
>
> — *Old Charleston epigram*

South Carolina's original inhabitants included the Catawba, Cherokee, and Yamasee. Colonial settlers from France and Great Britain began to arrive in the 1680s, as well as planters from Barbados, who brought with them enslaved Africans. German immigrants began to arrive in the 1730s, by which point African Americans made up 66 percent of the population. People from Wales, as well as Scotland and Ireland, began to arrive in the 1750s, the last of the large waves of immigration to the state.

Today, South Carolina has a population of 4,012,012, a 15 percent increase since 1990. Although the majority of the population from 1820 to 1920 was African-American, in the first half of the twentieth century many African Americans moved north. Their departure meant that the state's rate of population growth was much slower than that of most other states in the nation at that time.

Age Distribution in South Carolina (2000 Census)	
0–4	264,679
5–19	871,099
20–24	281,714
25–44	1,185,955
45–64	923,232
65 & over	485,333

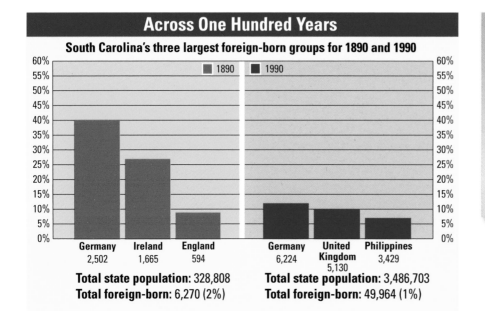

Across One Hundred Years

South Carolina's three largest foreign-born groups for 1890 and 1990

■ 1890 ■ 1990

| Germany 2,502 | Ireland 1,665 | England 594 | Germany 6,224 | United Kingdom 5,130 | Philippines 3,429 |

Total state population: 328,808
Total foreign-born: 6,270 (2%)

Total state population: 3,486,703
Total foreign-born: 49,964 (1%)

Patterns of Immigration

The total number of people who immigrated to South Carolina in 1998 was 2,125. Of that number, the largest immigrant groups were from Mexico (12.2%), India (8.6%), and Colombia (5.2%).

In contrast to the state's early years, when each decade brought a new influx of immigrants, almost 75 percent of the state's population today is not just native to the United States, but native to South Carolina as well. The median age of the population is 35.4, up from 31.9 in 1990 — almost exactly the same as the 35.3 national average.

Where They Live

South Carolinians are fairly equally divided between urban and rural areas, with about 54.6 percent living in cities and 45.4 percent living in rural areas. In 2000, the average population density was 133 people per square mile (51 per sq km). The largest city is the capital, Columbia, at 116,278 residents. Other major urban centers include the port of Charleston, North Charleston, industrial Greenville, Rock Hill, Mount Pleasant, and Spartanburg, a textile and railroad center. For much of the state's history, the majority

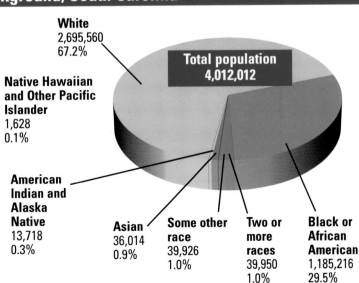

Heritage and Background, South Carolina   Year 2000

▶ Here's a look at the racial backgrounds of South Carolinians today. South Carolina ranks fourth among all U.S. states with regard to African Americans as a percentage of the population.

White
2,695,560
67.2%

Native Hawaiian and Other Pacific Islander
1,628
0.1%

American Indian and Alaska Native
13,718
0.3%

Asian
36,014
0.9%

Some other race
39,926
1.0%

Two or more races
39,950
1.0%

Black or African American
1,185,216
29.5%

Total population 4,012,012

Note: 2.4% (95,076) of the population identify themselves as **Hispanic** or **Latino,** a cultural designation that crosses racial lines. Hispanics and Latinos are counted in this category, as well as the racial category of their choice.

of the population lived in rural areas. Urbanization took place largely in the latter half of the twentieth century.

Education

South Carolina has a long history in public education. As early as 1710, the colonial assembly passed laws for the education of the needy, and the first school for African-American children was established in 1740. Laws for a public education system in South Carolina were passed in 1811, but public education wasn't guaranteed until the 1868 Reconstruction Constitution. Schools improved during the twentieth century. Most funds, however, were directed to schools for white children. When the U.S. Supreme Court ruled in 1954 that segregation was unconstitutional, South Carolina was slow to comply. The state attempted to delay desegregation in 1955 by repealing a 1937 law that made school compulsory for children between the ages of eight and fourteen. The law was reinstated in 1967.

Today, South Carolinians between the ages of five and seventeen must attend school. While 78.7 percent of workers twenty-five years or older have attained a high school diploma or higher, the state ranks fiftieth in terms of high school-age students who graduate, at 53.2 percent, compared to the U.S. average of 67.8 percent.

Love of Libraries

In colonial days, the South Carolina assembly broke new ground by being the first to give government funds to aid libraries. The University of South Carolina (USC) is home to the first building in the United States to be used exclusively as a free-standing college library. Built in 1840, the building was the main library at USC until 1940. Today, it is named the South Caroliniana Library.

▼ The architecture of Charleston still retains much of its antebellum, or pre-Civil War, flavor.

Educational Levels of South Carolina Workers (age 25 and over)	
Less than 9th grade	295,167
9th to 12th grade, no diploma	392,093
High school graduate, including equivalency	639,358
Some college, no degree or associate degree	480,139
Bachelor's degree	243,161
Graduate or professional degree	117,672

The oldest institution of higher education in the state (and the oldest municipal college in the country) is the College of Charleston, founded in 1770. The school became a part of the state college system in 1970. The largest institution of higher learning is the University of South Carolina at Columbia, founded in 1801. The Citadel is a well-known state-supported military college in Charleston. There are a total of thirty-three public and twenty-nine private institutions in the state. Other leading institutions include the Medical University of South Carolina, Clemson University, Bob Jones University, Limestone College, and Columbia College.

Religion

More than 73 percent of South Carolinians are Christian. Nearly 50 percent of the population are Baptist. At 15.6 percent, Methodists are the second-largest group. Other Protestant denominations, including Presbyterians (3.5 percent), Episcopalians (2 percent), and Pentecostals (2 percent), are present in smaller numbers. Roman Catholics comprise 5.7 percent of the state's population. The state is also home to Unitarian congregations, as well as smaller evangelical and fundamentalist groups. Founded in 1820 by Pope Pius VII, the Diocese of Charleston is one of the oldest Catholic dioceses in the United States. South Carolina was the first state to allow Jews to vote, and by 1800 the state had the largest Jewish population in the nation. Today, Jews make up about 0.2 percent of the population. About 0.2 percent of the population are Muslim, and about 0.1 percent are Buddhist.

From the Mountains to the Sea

> Nowhere else in the world has nature been so kind to her children as in those regions where the plantations were formed out of the Edenlike wilderness of the Low-Country.
>
> — *Archibald Rutledge,* The Carolina Low-Country, *1931*

South Carolina has a varied landscape — from the Spanish moss-draped ancient oaks and misty swamps of the Low Country to the Up Country's rugged mountains and hardwood forests.

Rivers and Lakes

South Carolina does not have any significant natural lakes, but several large lakes were formed in the 1930s and 1940s by the construction of dams on major rivers. These artificially-created lakes include Lake Marion, Lake Moultrie, and Lake Murray. Much to the delight of fishing enthusiasts, the forested land that now lies below the surface of these lakes creates excellent habitats for bluegills, striped bass, catfish, and crappies.

The state has three major river systems: the Pee Dee, Santee, and Savannah, all flowing from the northwest to the southeast. While all three systems have been used as water "highways," none of the rivers is navigable beyond the coastal plains because of the fall line that divides the state into Low Country and Up Country. Fall lines mark the division between an upland area and a coastal plain.

Highest Point
Sassafras Mountain
3,560 feet (1,085 m)
above sea level

▼ *From left to right:* the Grand Strand; Kiawah Island; the rugged Up Country; the yellow warbler, a South Carolina native; Lake Jocassee; cotton growing in the Piedmont region.

At the fall line, there are waterfalls and rapids that boats cannot cross.

Mountains and Valleys

The Up Country lies above the fall line in the northwestern section of the state. Here, the reddish soil and rock outcroppings of the rolling hills of the Piedmont Plateau give way to the Blue Ridge Mountains in the state's northwestern corner. The Piedmont region rises from 490 feet (150 m) to 985 feet (300 m). The Blue Ridge Mountains are part of the Appalachian Mountain system that stretches from Maine to Georgia.

Coastal Plains

The Low Country, or Atlantic Coastal Plain, covers about two-thirds of the state. Along the ocean are the Grand Strand beaches, numerous salt marshes, and sounds, as well as the Sea Islands to the south. Farther inland are cypress swamps, the Pine Barrens, and the Sand Hills. The outer Coastal Plain is generally forested, with most agriculture found in the inner Coastal Plain. Visitors flock to coastal resorts such as Hilton Head and Kiawah Island to enjoy the beaches. The origin of the many egg-shaped bays along South Carolina's coast continues to puzzle scientists. The bays may have been formed by a meteor hitting Earth or by the area's prevailing southwesterly winds.

Plants and Animals

The state mammal, the white-tailed deer, is found statewide. Recent programs to increase the size and number of forests in the state have contributed to the increase in their population. Other animals found in the state include opossums, beavers, alligators, and rabbits. Waterfowl are found in large numbers, particularly during

Average January temperature
Charleston: 48.5°F (9.2°C)
Columbia: 45.5°F (7.5°C)

Average July temperature
Charleston: 80°F (26.7°C)
Columbia: 81°F (27.2°C)

Average yearly rainfall
Charleston: 52 inches (132 centimeters)
Columbia: 46 inches (117 cm)

Average yearly snowfall
Charleston: 0.6 inches (1.5 cm)
Columbia: 1.7 inches (4.3 cm)

DID YOU KNOW?

In Charles Town, April 1737, the first systematic, scientific recording of the weather was made by Dr. John Lining. He recorded temperature, rainfall, atmospheric pressure, humidity, wind direction, and wind speed three times a day.

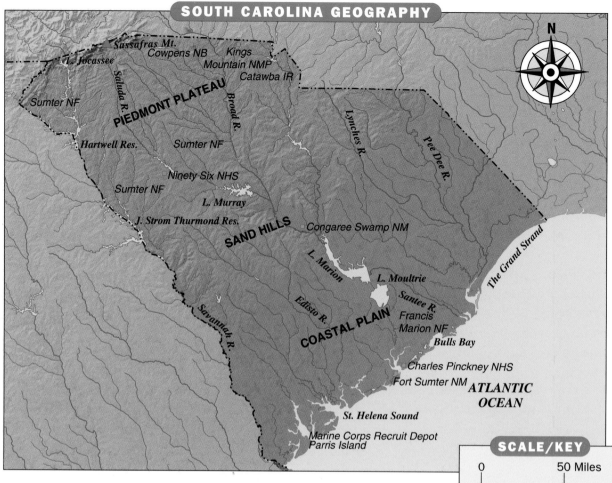

Sassafras Mt.
Cowpens NB
Kings Mountain NMP
Catawba IR
L. Jocassee
Saluda R.
PIEDMONT PLATEAU
Broad R.
Sumter NF
Hartwell Res.
Sumter NF
Lynches R.
Pee Dee R.
Ninety Six NHS
Sumter NF
L. Murray
J. Strom Thurmond Res.
SAND HILLS
Congaree Swamp NM
L. Marion
L. Moultrie
Savannah R.
Edisto R.
COASTAL PLAIN
Santee R.
Francis Marion NF
The Grand Strand
Bulls Bay
Charles Pinckney NHS
Fort Sumter NM
ATLANTIC OCEAN
St. Helena Sound
Marine Corps Recruit Depot Parris Island

SCALE/KEY

| 0 | 50 Miles |
| 0 | 50 Kilometers |

IR — Indian Reservation
NB — National Battlefield
NF — National Forest
NHS — National Historic Site
NM — National Monument
NMP — National Military Park
▲ — Highest Point
— Mountains

spring and fall migration. Birds such as the ruffed grouse, mockingbird, catbird, and yellow warbler are common inland. Freshwater fishing for bass, bluegills, crappies, and trout is popular in the lakes and rivers, while clams, oysters, shrimp, and shad are found along the coast.

South Carolina's plant life is as diverse as its animal life. Large pines, gums, live oaks, cypresses, and magnolias are found near the coast and on the Sea Islands. The state tree, the palmetto, also grows along the coast, as does the Spanish moss that cloaks the tree limbs. Live oaks grow to great size, and their tough wood was long used in shipbuilding. A wild grass called sea oats helps protect the coast from erosion by clinging to the sand dunes. Farther inland are the rushes, cattails, and grasses of the freshwater marshes, and the dwarf palmettos, loblolly pines, and water oaks of the sand hills. The sand hills are areas of rolling hills covered in sand and hardy plants. The quick-growing loblolly pine is most common in the former cotton fields of the Piedmont region. Oak and hickory are indigenous to the area, and flowering dogwoods, tulip trees, sourwoods, and mountain azaleas adorn the countryside. Hardwood forests are found in the Blue Ridge Mountains.

Natural Resources

The Santee and Savannah River systems provide the state with abundant hydroelectric power. Minerals found in the state include vermiculite, sand, kaolin (white clay), gravel, mica, and gemstones such as amethysts. South Carolina is the only gold-producing state east of the Mississippi River.

Climate

South Carolina has a humid subtropical climate, except in the Blue Ridge Mountains in the northwestern section of the state. Climatologists and geologists designate this region as humid continental. The coastal region is warmed by the Gulf Stream, which brings warm, humid air inland in the winter. Snowfall is infrequent, occurring most often in the mountains. In general, the heaviest precipitation occurs in late winter and in summer.

Tropical cyclones, better known as hurricanes, have been known to pummel the South Carolina coast in late summer and early fall. The state also has a tornado season, which occurs from February through September, with peak periods in May and August.

Major Rivers

Savannah River
314 miles (505 km)

Edisto River
244 miles (393 km)

Pee Dee River
166 miles (267 km)

Largest Lakes

Lake Marion
110,000 acres
(44,517 ha)

Lake Moultrie
60,000 acres (24,282 ha)

Lake Murray
50,000 acres (20,235 ha)

▼ Table Rock Mountain in northwestern South Carolina.

Making a Living in South Carolina

> More than any other state of the Confederacy, South Carolina has seemed to the rushing industrial regions of the United States "a land of monuments and memories."
> — The New York Times, *1930*

South Carolina came late to industrial expansion, and when manufacturing did come to the forefront in the twentieth century, it was built on the state's agricultural resources. The Piedmont clothing industry, for example, depended on the state's cotton crop. For the most part, textile mill jobs commanded only low wages. While agriculture remains a mainstay of the state's revenue today, manufacturing, from chemicals to automobiles, now drives the state's economic engine, as do tourism and forestry. Federal military posts are also major employers in the state, with facilities at Fort Jackson in Columbia, the Marine Corps Recruit Depot at Parris Island, and an air force base in Charleston. Low taxes make the state attractive to foreign investors, as well as to companies from other states.

Services

Service industry jobs account for the largest single group of workers in the state. Jobs in this sector include positions in the tourist industry, including hotel and restaurant workers, and a variety of careers in fields such as law, medicine, and education. Food service industry jobs are closely connected to the state's agricultural sector and include beverage bottling, food processing, and packaging.

Agriculture

Agriculture in South Carolina is a $1.2 billion-per-year business. Some twenty-four thousand farms produce everything from tobacco to soybeans to beef, with an

Top Employers
(of workers age sixteen and over)

Services	28.2%
Manufacturing	25.7%
Wholesale and retail trade	20.2%
Construction	7.9%
Finance, insurance, and real estate	5.1%
Public Administration	4.5%
Transportation, communications, and other public utilities	2.2%
Agriculture, forestry, and fisheries	2.2%
Mining	0.1%

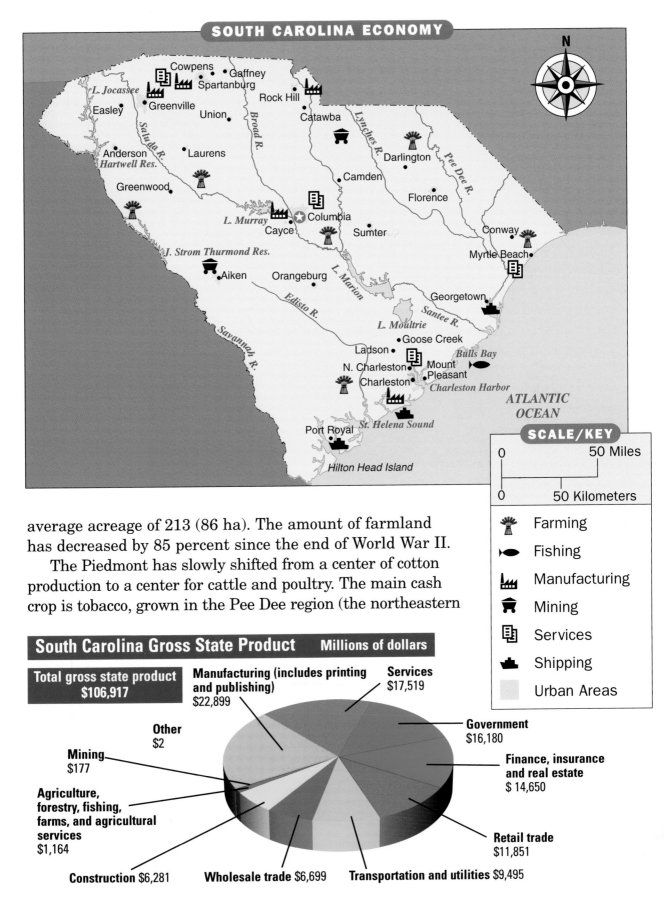

SOUTH CAROLINA ECONOMY

average acreage of 213 (86 ha). The amount of farmland has decreased by 85 percent since the end of World War II.

The Piedmont has slowly shifted from a center of cotton production to a center for cattle and poultry. The main cash crop is tobacco, grown in the Pee Dee region (the northeastern

South Carolina Gross State Product — Millions of dollars

Total gross state product $106,917

- Manufacturing (includes printing and publishing) $22,899
- Services $17,519
- Government $16,180
- Finance, insurance and real estate $ 14,650
- Retail trade $11,851
- Transportation and utilities $9,495
- Wholesale trade $6,699
- Construction $6,281
- Agriculture, forestry, fishing, farms, and agricultural services $1,164
- Mining $177
- Other $2

SCALE/KEY

0 — 50 Miles
0 — 50 Kilometers

- Farming
- Fishing
- Manufacturing
- Mining
- Services
- Shipping
- Urban Areas

section of the Coastal Plains), while the leading crop in acreage is soybeans.

Although Georgia is known as the "Peach State," peaches play a strong role in the agriculture of South Carolina as well. Only California produces more peaches. Other important agricultural products include dairy products, hogs, wheat, oats, barley, tomatoes, beans, peanuts, and cotton.

Manufacturing

Textile manufacturing, while in decline, is still the state's leading industry. South Carolina ranks third only to North Carolina and Georgia in textile production. The production of chemicals is becoming increasingly important to South Carolina's economy. Chemicals made in the state include agricultural fertilizers, pharmaceuticals, and synthetic fibers. Industrial machinery, rubber and plastics, electronic equipment, and paper are among the other industrial products in the state. Manufacturing centers are found in the Piedmont region, and industrial hot spots in the state include Charleston, Columbia, Greenville, Rock Hill, and Spartanburg.

Natural Resources, Forestry, Fishing

The balmy climate, broad sandy beaches, and forests that cover 65 percent of the state combine to enrich the lives of South Carolinians and visitors alike. Out of these resources, lumber and pulpwood industries have grown, as has the $29.3 million-a-year fishing industry. The timber harvested from the forests is mainly softwoods, such as the loblolly pine. The wood from these trees is used for lumber and paper. The coastal fishing industry's catch includes shrimp, blue crabs, oysters, and clams as the main sources of revenue.

Tourism

The state's mild weather makes it a year-round destination for tourists, who are particularly drawn to the coast. The $4.5 billion tourist industry has been on the rise in recent years, with shopping, hiking, boating, and other outdoor activities topping the list. Other attractions in the state include historic sites, museums, and numerous golf courses. There are more than forty state parks and several national historic sites and monuments, including Ninety Six National Historic Site and Fort Sumter National Monument.

**Made in
South Carolina**

**Leading farm products
and crops**
Tobacco
Soybeans
Peaches
Livestock
Cotton
Poultry
Dairy Products
Hogs
Grains
Tomatoes
Beans
Peanuts

Other products
Apparel and textiles
Chemicals
Industrial machinery
Paper
Wood products
Metal products
Rubber
Plastics
Electronics

Mining

Some five hundred mines operate in the state of South Carolina. Mineral deposits, such as sand, clay, gravel, and gold are found in the state and contribute to the $425 million mining industry. Aiken leads the country in kaolin production, a white clay used in ceramics and in medicine, and vermiculite, which is often used in lightweight concrete and plaster production. The state is also a leader in the production of mica, used in electronics, and marl, which is often used in fertilizer. Production of granite and limestone, both of which are used in construction, is also significant.

Transportation

South Carolina has an impressive and extensive highway system, 754 miles (1,213 km) of which are interstates. Railroads are less important today than they once were, but the ports of Charleston, Georgetown, and Port Royal still ship large amounts of freight for the state. South Carolina's location along the Atlantic Intracoastal Waterway accounts for the heavy shipping. The Atlantic Intracoastal Waterway, a system of 1,200 miles (1,931 km) of water routes, connects ports from Massachusetts to Florida. Part of the route was created by digging canals to link natural waterways. The waterway is used primarily for commerce in its northern sections and more for recreation in South Carolina. During World War II, the waterway provided an invaluable means for U.S. ships to avoid attacks by German submarines that lurked off the Atlantic coast.

Major airports serve Charleston, Columbia, Greenville-Spartanburg, and the Myrtle Beach resort area, and there is a network of smaller regional airports as well.

▲ Beautiful scenery draws tourists to South Carolina. On Hilton Head Island, famous for its golf courses, more than 60 percent of jobs are connected to tourism.

Major Airports		
Airport	**Location**	**Passengers per year (2000)**
Charleston International	Charleston	1,676,710
Myrtle Beach International	Myrtle Beach	1,582,372
Greenville-Spartanburg International	Greenville	1,412,567
Columbia Metro	Columbia	1,201,524

Independent State of Mind

> The very essence of a free government consists in considering offices as public trusts, bestowed for the good of the country, and not for the benefit of an individual or a party.
>
> — *John C. Calhoun, South Carolina senator, 1835*

S outh Carolina was a recognized Royal Colony from 1729 until 1776, when an independent government was formed. In 1788, South Carolina became the eighth state to ratify the U.S. Constitution. The state charter was adopted in 1790, replacing the royal charter.

Republican Abraham Lincoln's election in 1860 put a spotlight on the conflict over slavery that had been brewing for thirty years. On December 20, 1860, South Carolina became the first state to secede from the Union. Subsequently, the state suffered politically, socially, and economically through the Civil War and Reconstruction periods, and it was occupied by federal troops from 1866 to 1877. It wasn't until South Carolina adopted the Constitution of 1868, which established universal male suffrage and abolished the requirement that a man had to have property to hold office, that it would regain admittance to the Union.

The state's 1895 constitution was revised in the early 1970s. The executive, the legislative, and the judicial are the three main branches of state government. The state has eight electoral votes in presidential elections, two U.S. senators, and six congressional representatives.

The Executive Branch

South Carolina's governor is the head of the executive branch. The governor has the power to propose legislation and budgets, to appoint some cabinet members, and to veto legislation. The governor is elected for a four-year term, and can serve only two consecutive terms. Other elected

Ernest A. Finney, Jr.

B orn in 1931 in Smithfield, Virginia, Ernest Finney graduated from South Carolina State College's School of Law in 1954, but he was unable to practice law at first — African-American lawyers were not admitted to the state lawyers' association at the time. In 1960, he began full-time practice as a lawyer, and he eventually handled civil rights cases for more than 6,000 clients. Finney lost almost every case in the lower courts because South Carolina law still protected segregation, but he won all but two of the cases on appeal, a remarkable record. In 1994, the South Carolina General Assembly elected him as the first African-American chief justice of the state's supreme court since Reconstruction.

Elected Posts in the Executive Branch

Office	Length of Term	Term Limits
Governor	4 years	2 consecutive terms
Lieutenant Governor	4 years	None
Secretary of State	4 years	None
Attorney General	4 years	None
Comptroller General	4 years	None
Treasurer	4 years	None
State Superintendent of Education	4 years	None
Commissioner of Agriculture	4 years	None
Adjutant General	4 years	None

officials in the executive branch are the lieutenant governor, who is second in command; the secretary of state, who keeps the records of the state; the attorney general, who represents the state in legal cases; and the comptroller general and the treasurer, who oversee the collection and

▼ Construction on the state capitol building in Columbia began in 1851. Because of a series of arguments with architects and the intervention of the Civil War, the capitol was not completed until 1911.

distribution of state funds. In addition, the state superintendent of education, the commissioner of agriculture, and the adjutant general, who is the head of the state's military, are elected officers in the executive branch. In 1993, the legislature reorganized state agencies into eleven departments, giving the governor the right to appoint cabinet secretaries to run the agencies.

The Legislative Branch

South Carolina's legislative branch, called the General Assembly, is divided into two parts, the senate and the house of representatives. There are 46 senators and 124 representatives in the General Assembly, each representing either a senate or a representative electoral district. Senators are elected for four-year terms, while representatives are elected for two-year terms. Neither body has term limits. The assembly meets from January through June each year. Any member may propose a bill, which is reviewed by committee, sometimes revised, and then voted on by the entire body. After the bill has passed, it is sent to the other assembly body (that is, the house sends it to the senate and vice versa), where it undergoes the same process before being sent to the governor, who must sign the bill for it to become a law.

The Judicial Branch

The supreme court, composed of one chief justice and four associate justices, is the highest court in the state judicial system. The General Assembly elects the justices to ten-year terms, staggered so that an election is required every two years. A case comes before the supreme court when a plaintiff (person bringing a case) is unhappy with the decision of a lower court and appeals to the supreme court for a new decision. The supreme court also hears cases involving the death penalty, elections, or the constitutionality of laws.

General Assembly			
House	Number of Members	Length of Term	Term Limits
Senate	46 senators	4 years	None
House of Representatives	124 representatives	2 years	None

The White House via South Carolina

Andrew Jackson (1829–1837)

Born March 15, 1767, in a settlement in Waxhaw, South Carolina, Andrew Jackson was the first U.S. president to have been born in a log cabin. Jackson's political career began in 1796 in Tennessee, when he became the first Republican in that state elected to the U.S. House of Representatives. He served briefly in the Senate and became a hero for his role in defeating the British at New Orleans in the War of 1812. His heroism helped him win the presidency in 1828.

As president, Jackson supported eliminating the Electoral College and democratizing federal office-holding — ideas that were not popular with Congress. Jackson's policies eventually led to later conflicts that would lead to secession and civil war in the 1860s.

Woodrow Wilson (1913–1921)

Woodrow Wilson was born in Virginia in 1856, but during his youth he lived in Columbia, South Carolina, because his father was a professor there. As president, Wilson introduced a graduated federal tax system, the Federal Reserve Act, and the Federal Trade Commission. Later he proposed child labor laws and a restriction of eight-hour days for railroad workers. After leading the nation through its involvement in World War I, Wilson helped to create the League of Nations, which eventually became the United Nations.

The court of appeals was created in 1983 to hear most appeals from the family or circuit courts, unless the appeal involves one of the classes of jurisdiction directly under the supreme court. A chief judge and eight associate judges serve on the court, elected to staggered terms of six years each. The court of appeals can hear arguments and motions from any county in the state, either as a whole or in three panels of three judges each.

The circuit court has a civil court (court of common pleas) and a criminal court (court of general sessions). The state is divided into sixteen judicial circuits, with forty-six circuit judges who serve on a rotating basis. Circuit court judges are elected by the General Assembly for terms of six years.

DID YOU KNOW?

In 1996, Governor David Beasley proposed removing the Confederate flag from the State House. His proposal sparked a statewide controversy. To some Southerners, the flag represents Southern pride, while to others it stands for a history of racism. The flag was finally removed in 2000.

A Presence Touched by the Past

In Charleston, more than elsewhere,
you get the feeling that the twentieth
century is a vast, unconscionable mistake.

— *Pat Conroy, U.S. author,*
The Lords of Discipline, *1980.*

South Carolinians, much like southern Californians, like to boast that you can enjoy the state's mountains in the morning and the ocean in the evening. A mild climate encourages South Carolinians to enjoy a vast and sometimes surprising array of outdoor activities, including surfing, scuba diving, canoeing, kayaking, rafting, fishing, shrimping, crabbing, hunting, and hiking. Golf and tennis are also popular pastimes. South Carolina has more than forty state parks, several national wildlife refuges, and two national forests, offering a wide variety of places in which to enjoy nature and learn more about South Carolina's ecology and history.

▼ Myrtle Beach is one of the state's most famous attractions.

The Congaree Swamp National Monument in Hopkins is not a true swamp, but rather a large forest in a floodplain. Trees in this forest are among the tallest in the East and have some of the highest leaf canopies in the world. Visitors can walk through the park on boardwalks, marveling at one of the oldest intact forests in the nation. Santee State Park, on the banks of Lake Marion, is a popular place for fishermen and others who enjoy spending time on or in the water. The park offers boat tours of the lake that introduce visitors to its abundant wildlife.

Hilton Head and the Grand Strand beaches, such as Myrtle Beach, are especially busy during spring, when chilly northerners come south for an early taste of summer.

Historical Sites

South Carolina holds its history dear, as is evidenced by the numerous Revolutionary War and Civil War sites around the state. Cowpens National Battlefield is the site of a pivotal battle in the American Revolution. On this site in 1781, Daniel Morgan led troops of the Continental Army against British troops under the command of Banastre Tarleton. Morgan's men prevailed and turned the tide of the war in the south, making the colonists' victory possible.

The Fort Sumter National Monument, which stands at the end of a small spit of land jutting into the ocean, was the site of the first battle of the Civil War. Union troops held out for thirty-four hours but finally surrendered to Confederate attacks. Union forces then battered the fort for almost two years while the Confederates held it.

Plantations in their antebellum splendor are another historical draw. Charleston's Magnolia Plantation and Middleton Place are known for their gardens. Magnolia's newest addition is the Audubon Swamp Garden. The artist John Audubon, famous for his paintings of birds, once visited the plantation as a guest of Dr. Charles Drayton. Middleton has the oldest landscaped gardens in the United States, started in the 1740s. Visitors can tour an early Georgian plantation house at North Charleston's Drayton Hall, while Boone Hall Plantation in Mount Pleasant has been completely reconstructed and is the site of summertime battle reenactments.

▲ The terraced gardens of Middleton Place were once part of a large plantation. They are the oldest landscaped gardens in the United States.

DID YOU KNOW?

The Dock Street Theatre in Charleston opened in 1736 and may have been the site of the first play produced in the thirteen colonies.

Beaufort, Georgetown, Camden, and Charleston boast some of the best-preserved colonial historic districts in America, and many other smaller towns have preserved the flavor of the past in their architecture and often in their customs. The Battery district in Charleston is the site of some of the finest antebellum homes in the nation.

The Rice Museum in Georgetown and the Florence Air and Missile Museum celebrate important elements of South Carolina's economic history.

Museums and the Arts

South Carolina has many art museums. Some historical South Carolina collections include those of The Charleston Museum, the oldest museum in the United States; the Old Slave Mart Museum; and the South Carolina State Museum at Columbia, which, among other exhibits, showcases contemporary South Carolina artists. The Old Slave Mart Museum in Charleston is housed in a building constructed in 1859 and used for the sale of slaves, which was once a profitable business in the city. Before 1856, slaves were sold at open markets, but a law passed that year required that the markets be held indoors. The Old Slave Mart, which is the only such structure still standing in the state, was constructed by Thomas Ryan and was known as Ryan's Mart. The building's main hall had a 20-foot (6-m) ceiling and 3-foot (0.9-m) high tables, on which African-American men and women stood so they could be inspected by prospective buyers. The building now repudiates its grim past by housing a collection that

◀ This figure is one of many intriguing pieces of twentieth-century sculpture that grace the grounds of Brookgreen Gardens in northeastern South Carolina, between Myrtle Beach and Georgetown.

celebrates African-American history, arts, and crafts. Charleston's Gibbes Museum features important eighteenth- and nineteenth-century portraiture by colonial artists such as Henrietta Johnson and miniaturist Charles Fraser. In Greenville, the Bob Jones University Museum & Gallery houses an impressive collection of Old Masters, including Titian, Rembrandt, Rubens, and Van Dyck. The Brookgreen Gardens, south of Myrtle Beach, exhibits nineteenth- and twentieth-century sculpture in an outdoor setting.

The work of South Carolina native Jasper Johns, one of the most famous contemporary artists from the state, is exhibited in museum collections around the world.

Each year Charleston celebrates the arts with the seventeen-day long Spoleto festival. The festival is modeled on one that takes place in Spoleto, Italy, and draws attention to the talents of young artists in many media. Performances at the festival include ballet, modern dance, opera, jazz, classical music, and theater. In addition, writers read their works aloud and galleries hold exhibits of new artists. The festival, which takes place in late May and early June, draws artists and audiences from around the world.

A Literary Tradition

Reflecting its complex social history, South Carolina has always had storytellers. While many stories were passed down through an oral tradition or through music, the state also has had its share of published authors. William Gilmore Simms (1806–1876) was a writer of historical romances set in the antebellum South. Mary Boykin Chesnut (1823–1886) was a famous Civil War diarist. Julia Peterkin won the 1929 Pulitzer Prize for her book *Scarlet Sister Mary,* about plantation life from a Gullah woman's perspective. The state's first poet laureate, Archibald Rutledge, held the title for thirty-nine years. DuBose Heyward, also a South Carolinian, wrote *Porgy* (1925), which became the basis for George Gershwin's opera *Porgy and Bess* (1935).

Famous contemporary writers include poet James Dickey, who was a University of South Carolina professor and author of the book *Deliverance*; William Price Fox; and Pat Conroy of Beaufort, the best-selling author of *The Prince of Tides* and *The Great Santini.*

▲ William Gilmore Simms, author of *The Sack and Destruction of Columbia, South Carolina* (1865).

Cut a *what*?

Shag clubs are popular in South Carolina, with one in practically every medium- to large-sized town. "Shaggers" gather regularly to "cut a rug" (dance) and enjoy "beach music." Beach music was originally rhythm and blues but expanded into other styles later, the requirement being that you can "shag" to it. Ocean Drive Beach is where teenagers on summer break invented shagging in the 1950s. The step is a hybrid of the jitterbug and the lindy hop. Shag music, which is generally four beats to the measure, is typified by hits such as "60 Minute Man" and "Under the Boardwalk."

Gullah Culture

"Gullah" refers to the descendants of slaves living on South Carolina's Sea Islands. Having lived there in relative isolation for generations, they developed a Creole language, which is a hybrid of English and African languages. Most of the slaves in colonial North America came from countries in West Africa, sometimes via the West Indies. The slaves brought with them skills such as carpentry, iron working, rice cultivation, and basket weaving. Baskets, called fanners, were first woven by slaves out of palmetto, rushes, or white oak and used to winnow, or sift, rice at plantations. Now often made out of softer sea grass, fanners are still made today, bearing a striking resemblance to the African baskets found in Angola and Senegal. Storytelling is another enduring Gullah art form, with many tales of African origin, such as "B'rer Rabbit" (later popularized by Joel Chandler Harris). The York W. Bailey Museum at the Penn Center on St. Helena Island is dedicated to preserving Gullah history and culture. The Penn Center is a dedicated National Historic Landmark District. It was the site of the first school for freed slaves in the South. Dr. Martin Luther King, Jr., and his Southern Christian Leadership Conference planned their civil rights campaigns there in the late 1950s and 1960s.

▲ A South Carolinian woman demonstrates traditional Gullah methods of basket-making using sea grass.

A Variety of Beats

As in much of the deep South, music has played a huge role in South Carolina's culture, with enormous variety in the musical tradition found within the state. Country, rap, bluegrass, gospel, jazz, rock, beach music, and rhythm and blues are all represented in clubs and other live music venues. Charleston and Beaufort are great places to enjoy live jazz; Spartanburg has nurtured country-rock stars such as members of the Marshall Tucker Band and legendary bluegrass guitarist Alvin "Pink" Anderson. Country star Aaron Tippin, the son of an Up Country farmer, hails from Greenville. Other famous South Carolinian musicians include James Brown, the "Godfather of Soul"; Chubby Checker, who wrote "The Twist"; torch singer Eartha Kitt; and jazz great Dizzy Gillespie. Charleston, Columbia, Spartanburg, Myrtle Beach, and Greenville all have symphony orchestras.

DID YOU KNOW?

South Carolina is no stranger to Hollywood — *The Great Santini, The Big Chill, Forrest Gump, The Prince of Tides,* and *Rich in Love* were novels set in the state. They were later turned into movies filmed on location in the state.

Sports

While there are no major league sports teams in South Carolina, the minor leagues are well supported by fans. College football takes on a seriousness of its own in the state, with fans mainly divided regionally between the University of South Carolina Gamecocks and the Clemson University Tigers. As in much of the South, NASCAR (National Association of Stock Car Auto Racing) races are a popular spectator sport, with the Darlington Raceway as the site for the NASCAR TranSouth Financial 400 stock car race each spring and the Mountain Dew Southern 500 on Labor Day. The National Motorsports Press Association Stock Car Hall of Fame is located next to the raceway in Darlington. Horseracing is also popular in South Carolina. Aiken hosts the Aiken Triple Crown Horse Races over three weekends in March, and Camden holds the Colonial Cup steeplechase race each November.

South Carolina has produced many star athletes. "Shoeless" Joe Jackson, born in Brandon Mills, was one of the greatest baseball players of his day, excelling equally in hitting and fielding. Jackson grew up playing baseball for the team of the cotton mill where he worked from an early age. In 1919, he was a member of the Chicago White Sox team that was favored to win the World Series. In a scandal that shocked the nation, the team was found to have accepted bribes to lose the series. Jackson and his teammates were banned from baseball, and he was never inducted into the Hall of Fame.

Larry Doby was another famous South Carolinian baseball player. Doby was the first African American to enter the American League and only the second African American, after Jackie Robinson, to play major league baseball.

Althea Gibson, another South Carolina sports pioneer, was born near Sumter and became the first African-American woman to win the All-England championship event at Wimbledon, the world-famous British tennis tournament, in 1957.

▼ Clemson University forward Tomas Nagys takes a shot in the second round of the Atlantic Coast Conference tournament, March 9, 2001.

Carolina Inspiration

Never let me hear that the blood of the brave has been shed
in vain! No! It sends a cry down through all time.
— *Mary Boykin Chesnut, 1865*

Following are only a few of the thousands of people who were born, died, or spent much of their lives in South Carolina and made extraordinary contributions to the state and the nation.

MARY BOYKIN CHESNUT
AUTHOR

BORN: *March 31, 1823, Pleasant Hill*
DIED: *November 22, 1886, Camden*

Mary Boykin Miller, the daughter of Stephen Decatur Miller, a congressman, senator, and governor, married James Chesnut, Jr., the son of a wealthy plantation owner, in 1840. Her husband would eventually serve in the Provisional Congress of the Confederate States of America and achieve the rank of general in the Confederate army. From February 1861 to July 1865, Chesnut recorded the experiences she had accompanying her husband and entertaining the elite society of the Confederacy. Her diaries have been collected in a book titled *Mary Chesnut's Civil War.* The book is recognized as a keenly accurate portrayal of the South during the Civil War and one of the finest pieces of literature to come out of the Confederacy.

STROM THURMOND
POLITICIAN

BORN: *December 5, 1902, Edgefield*

Serving as state senator (elected 1933), governor (first elected in 1946), and U.S. senator (first elected as a write-in in 1954), J. (James) Strom Thurmond holds the record for the longest career in South Carolina politics. Thurmond also holds the record for the longest filibuster, a tactic used to delay or stop action on proposed legislation, in U.S. Senate history. Speaking out against a proposed civil rights bill in 1957, Thurmond talked for twenty-four hours and eighteen minutes. In 1964,

Thurmond switched from the Democratic party, which had been the traditional party of Southern politicians, to the Republican party. Thurmond helped Richard Nixon in his successful run for the presidency in 1968. In 1998, the United Service Organization awarded Thurmond the "Spirit of Hope" award for his patriotism and support of U.S. troops.

CHARLES HARD TOWNES
PHYSICIST

BORN: *July 28, 1915, Greenville*

Charles Hard Townes was educated at Furman and Duke Universities and the California Institute of Technology. From 1939 to 1947, he worked on radar for bombs at Bell Telephone Laboratories. Townes's later work was related to U.S. defense policy. Over the course of his career, he taught at Columbia University, Massachusetts Institute of Technology (MIT), and the University of California at Berkeley. At Columbia, he conducted research that led to the development of a working maser, a device that produces intense beams of high-frequency microwave radio waves. In 1955, Townes published *Microwave Spectroscopy* with physicist Arthur L. Schawlow. He and Russian physicists Nikolay Basov and Aleksandr Prokhorov were awarded the Nobel Prize for physics in 1964 for their work in quantum electronics.

DIZZY GILLESPIE
JAZZ TRUMPETER

BORN: *October 21, 1917, Cheraw*
DIED: *January 6, 1993, Englewood, NJ*

John Birks Gillespie began playing trumpet when he was fifteen. He attended the Laurinburg Institute in

North Carolina and went on to become one of the premier jazz trumpeters and big band leaders in America. Over the course of his career, Gillespie worked with Cab Calloway, Earl "Fatha" Hines, and many other great musicians. Gillespie and jazz saxophone player Charlie Parker created the form of jazz known as bop, or bebop. Two of Gillespie's most important pieces are "Bebop" and "Night in Tunisia." Gillespie was a serious composer and virtuoso performer with a lighthearted stage persona that endeared him to audiences around the world.

JAMES DICKEY
WRITER

BORN: *February 2, 1923, Atlanta, GA*
DIED: *January 19, 1997, Columbia*

James Lafayette Dickey's interest in language may have been sparked by listening to his father, a lawyer, read portions of legal cases aloud. He interrupted his studies at Clemson College to join the air force during World War II. Dickey fought in the Pacific, and when the war ended, he enrolled at Vanderbilt University in Tennessee, where he studied English and wrote poetry. Before he graduated, he had a poem published in a prestigious literary journal. He did graduate work at Rice University in Texas and Vanderbilt before returning to the air force in the Korean War. He came back to a university teaching position but soon left to take a job in advertising. In 1961, he turned full-time to poetry and received a year-long Guggenheim Fellowship to live in Italy. That same year, he published his first volume of poetry, *Into the Stone and Other Poems.* His 1964 volume of poetry, *The Buckdancer's Choice,* won the National Book Award in 1965. He served as poetry consultant to the Library of Congress from 1966 to 1968, a position that later became Poet Laureate. Although he is considered a poet, Dickey is perhaps best known for his novel *Deliverance* (1970). Like most of Dickey's writing, the novel is set in the South and describes a harrowing trip through the wilderness. From 1968 until his death, Dickey taught and was poet-in-residence at the University of South Carolina.

Eartha Kitt
SINGER/ACTRESS
BORN: *January 17, 1927, Columbia*

Born on a cotton plantation, Eartha Mae Kitt was sent away by her mother at age eight to live in Harlem with her aunt. Kitt began her career in the 1950s as a dancer with the Katherine Dunham Dance Troupe. While on their European tour, a Parisian nightclub owner discovered her. She became well known in Paris as a nightclub singer. Kitt was

subsequently in the Broadway show *New Faces of 1952,* appearing in the film version as well. In 1968, Kitt was blacklisted by many in the entertainment industry for speaking out against the Vietnam War, but she returned to the stage in 1974 with a concert at Carnegie Hall. Over the course of her career, she was nominated twice for a Grammy Award, twice for a Tony Award, and once for an Emmy. Kitt is known for her song "Santa Baby" and her portrayal of Catwoman in the *Batman* television series — as well as for her distinctive sultry voice.

Althea Gibson
TENNIS CHAMPION
BORN: *August 25, 1927, Silver*

Althea Gibson's distinguished tennis career began when she won the New York State African-American singles tennis championship at the age of fifteen. In 1957, she won the women's singles championship at Wimbledon in England; the women's clay court singles championship at River Forest, Illinois; and the U.S. national women's championship, which was played at Forest Hills, New York. Gibson won Wimbledon and the U.S. national titles again in 1958, then turned to exhibition tennis from 1959 to 1960. In 1971, Gibson was inducted into the National Lawn Tennis Hall of Fame. Gibson had a second career in professional golf, where she was also a true pioneer.

JASPER JOHNS
ARTIST

BORN: *May 15, 1930, Augusta, GA*

Jasper Johns, who grew up in Allendale and attended the University of South Carolina, is considered one of the most important twentieth-century U.S. painters. He diverged from the abstract expressionist movement of the mid-1950s with his thickly painted canvases representing familiar objects. The most famous of these are his American flags. The heavy use of paint in his early work presented the idea of art-as-object, which would influence modern painting as well as sculpture. Johns's later use of collage and wordplay on his canvases was the immediate forerunner to the pop art movement. The Whitney Museum of American Art in New York City gave him a comprehensive retrospective show in 1977. In 1988, he was awarded the Grand Prix at the Venice Biennale.

JAMES BROWN
SINGER

BORN: *May 3, 1933, Barnwell*

Nicknamed the "Godfather of Soul," James Brown was born in South Carolina and raised in Augusta, Georgia. After years in reform school for a robbery arrest and failed attempts at boxing and baseball careers, Brown joined a gospel group. He then became the leader of a rhythm-and-blues group called the Famous Flames. In subsequent years, fronting a group known as the J.B.s, Brown dominated rhythm-and-blues music and had pop hits with songs like "Say It Loud, I'm Black and I'm Proud" (1968). Over his lifetime, Brown has had more than one hundred hit singles. His soul-stirring, driving sound, funk innovations, and slick dance moves have had far-reaching influence in pop, rock, jazz, and even hip hop and rap in recent years. In 1986, Brown was inducted into the Rock and Roll Hall of Fame and, in 2000, into the Songwriters Hall of Fame. He has been awarded four Grammys and, in 1992, a Lifetime Achievement Grammy Award.

JESSE JACKSON
CIVIL RIGHTS LEADER

BORN: *October 8, 1941, Greenville*

Early in his civil rights career, Jesse Jackson was an associate of Martin Luther King, Jr. He became a Baptist minister in 1968. Throughout the 1960s and 1970s, Jackson worked with organizations such as Operation Breadbasket in Chicago and Operation PUSH (People United to Save Humanity), which tried to create economic opportunities for African Americans. By the 1980s, Jackson was nationally known as a civil rights leader. He ran for the 1984 and 1988 Democratic presidential nomination on behalf of the "Rainbow Coalition." During the Persian Gulf War in the 1990s, Jackson traveled to Iraq to help secure the release of hostages.

South Carolina
History At-A-Glance

1526
First settlement attempt by Europeans in present-day South Carolina, led by Spaniard Lucas Vasquez de Ayllon.

1566
Spanish settle on Parris Island; they remain until 1587.

1663
King Charles II charters Carolina land to eight Lords Proprietors.

1670
The Lords Proprietors lead a group of settlers from England and Barbados to Albemarle Point.

1712
North Carolina is ruled separately from South Carolina.

1718
The pirate Blackbeard threatens to attack Charles Town.

1739
Slave uprising at Stono River plantations is subdued by local militia.

1750s
Piedmont region settled.

1776
South Carolina sends four delegates to the Continental Congress in Philadelphia, and they sign the Declaration of Independence.

1780
The British occupy Charles Town and stay until 1782.

1786
State capital moves from Charleston to Columbia.

1788
South Carolina ratifies the U.S. Constitution, becoming eighth state in the Union.

1600   **1700**   **1800**

1492
Christopher Columbus comes to New World.

1607
Capt. John Smith and three ships land on Virginia coast and start first English settlement in New World — Jamestown.

1754–63
French and Indian War.

1773
Boston Tea Party.

1776
Declaration of Independence adopted July 4.

1777
Articles of Confederation adopted by Continental Congress.

1787
U.S. Constitution written.

1812–14
War of 1812.

United States
History At-A-Glance

1801
University of South Carolina is chartered.

1832
Nullification controversy takes place over whether South Carolina has the right to nullify federal tariffs.

1861
With ten other states, South Carolina forms the Confederate States of America. The Civil War begins April 12 at Fort Sumter.

1865
Union army's General Sherman invades South Carolina.

1868
South Carolina readmitted to the Union.

1877
South Carolina planters and merchants establish "Bourbon Rule."

1890s
Jim Crow laws reinforce racial segregation throughout South Carolina.

1911
Hurricane destroys rice plantations, which never recover.

1963
Desegregation of South Carolina schools begins.

1975
James Edwards is elected governor, the first Republican since Reconstruction.

1994
African-American Ernest Finney elected chief justice of the state's supreme court.

1996
Strom Thurmond becomes the longest-serving U.S. Senator in history.

1800   **1900**   **2000**

1848
Gold discovered in California draws eighty thousand prospectors in the 1849 Gold Rush.

1861–65
Civil War.

1869
Transcontinental railroad completed.

1917–18
U.S. involvement in World War I.

1929
Stock market crash ushers in Great Depression.

1941–45
U.S. involvement in World War II.

1950–53
U.S. fights in the Korean War.

1964–73
U.S. involvement in Vietnam War.

2000
George W. Bush wins the closest presidential election in history.

2001
A terrorist attack in which four hijacked airliners crash into New York City's World Trade Center, the Pentagon, and farmland in western Pennsylvania leaves thousands dead or injured.

▼ Wofford College in Spartanburg, around 1909.

Festivals and Fun for All

Check web site for exact date and directions.

Aiken Triple Crown, Aiken

Each March, Aiken hosts three weekends of thoroughbred horse racing events. Aiken is one of the training centers for the country's top horse racing farms. The Triple Crown is seen as a spring warm-up after a winter of training.

www.aiken.net/visit_us/equestrian.htm

Autumnfest, Columbia

This October festival features arts and crafts, live music, international food, and more. The award-winning festival is held on the grounds of the historic Hampton-Preston Mansion and the Robert Mills House.

www.columbiasc.net/city/city1ec.htm

Battle of Cowpens Reenactment, Cowpens

In January, a reenactment of this Revolutionary War battle takes place at Cowpens National Battlefield. The Battle of Cowpens is considered one of the most important victories over British forces in the Southern Campaign.

www.nps.gov/cowp

Blue Crab Festival, Little River

This large festival offers incredible crafts and seafood every May. Events and attractions include a children's area, a business expo, live music, and all the crab you can eat.

www.littleriverchamber.com

Chitlin' Strut, Salley

This festival offers chitlins, country music, and fireworks each November. Started in 1966 when the mayor realized the town needed money for new Christmas decorations, its popularity has grown exponentially — it drew 2,500 people in 1967 and 50,000 in 1999.

www.chitlinstrut.com

Gullah Festival, Beaufort

This May festival celebrates the Low Country's African-American culture. The festival's goal is to preserve Sea Island history for future generations. Featured events include local music, gospel singing, dance, crafts, folklore, storytelling, fine arts, basketry, homemade quilts, traditional games originating in Africa, boatbuilding, and Low Country cuisine.

www.gullahfestival.com

▶ A giant puppet theater is one of the many attractions at the Spoleto Festival in Charleston.

Lowcountry Cajun Festival, Charleston

This festival features spicy Cajun cooking, crawfish, and Zydeco music every April. Children's events include games, air jumps, face painting, and train rides.

www.ccprc.com/special.htm

NASCAR Winston Cup Series TranSouth Financial 400, Darlington

The best of the best stock car drivers compete at this annual event. Crowds of fans come to cheer (and party) at this famous raceway every March.

www.darlingtonraceway.com

Penn Center, St. Helena Island

The Penn Center is nestled on 50 acres (20 ha) designated as a National Historic Landmark. It is the only African-American historical landmark in the state.

www.angelfire.com/sc/jhstevens/penncenter.html

Plantation Days, Charleston

Crafts and foods from the eighteenth and nineteenth centuries are celebrated at this festival each November. Middleton Place hosts the annual event, which highlights the skills needed for plantation life.

www.charlestoncvb.com/events.jsp?month=10

South Carolina Festival of Roses, Orangeburg

This is a big April event with arts, crafts, and lots of roses. Activities include a moonwalk, a petting zoo, road and river races, a pageant, and golf, horseshoe, softball, and tennis tournaments.

www.festivalofroses.com

South Carolina Peach Festival, Gaffney

Held for ten days in July, this festival features sporting events, concerts, a parade, and, of course, peaches. For years, the festival has attracted top country recording artists. The event is known for its giant parade, pageants, and peach-related extravaganzas.

www.gaffney-sc.com/Peachfest.htm

South Carolina State Fair, Columbia

Held in October, this old-fashioned state fair features live music, food, and rides. Visitors can view competitive exhibits in the areas of agriculture, home and craft, and livestock.

www.scstatefair.org

Spoleto Festival USA, Charleston

This prestigious annual music and theater event, held in May and June, has a counterpart in Spoleto, Italy. The festival is dedicated to the promotion of young artists in all the performing arts, contemporary and innovative works, and the expansion of public appreciation for the arts. More than one hundred events are offered each year.

www.spoletousa.org

Wooden Boat Show, Georgetown

Wooden boat builders from across South Carolina compete here every October. The show features a boat exhibit, maritime arts and crafts, food, music, and the Maritime Gallery Crawl.

www.woodenboatshow.com/Welcome.htm

Books

Branch, Muriel Miller. *The Water Brought Us: The Story of the Gullah-Speaking People.* Orangeburg, SC: Sandlapper Publishing, 2000. A book about the history, culture, and daily life of the Gullah people of the Sea Islands.

Lyons, Mary E. *Catching the Fire: Philip Simmons, Blacksmith.* Boston, MA: Houghton Mifflin Co., 1997. Biography of a poor but industrious descendant of a slave, who studied with Charleston's leading blacksmith and ultimately became one of the country's most treasured artists. His gates and fences decorate the city of Charleston.

Mace, Nancy. *In the Company of Men: A Woman at The Citadel.* New York: Simon & Schuster, 2001. This book chronicles Nancy Mace's life as the first female cadet ever to graduate from The Citadel, Charleston's famed military college.

Meadows, James. *Jesse Jackson (Journey to Freedom).* Chanhassen, MN: Child's World, 2000. A biography of South Carolinian Jesse Jackson, focusing on his contributions to the Civil Rights movement.

Schraff, Anne. *Woodrow Wilson (United States Presidents).* Springfield, NJ: Enslow Publishers, Inc., 1998. A biography chronicling Wilson's childhood, political career, and presidency.

Web Sites

▶ The official state web site
www.myscgov.com

▶ The official web site of Columbia, the state capital
www.columbiasc.net

▶ City of Charleston's official web site
www.ci.charleston.sc.us

▶ South Carolina Historical Society
www.schistory.org

▶ A directory of South Carolina information
www.sciway.net